M *Is for* Mama
STUDY GUIDE

Abbie Halberstadt
Illustrations by Lindsay Long

HARVEST HOUSE PUBLISHERS
EUGENE. OREGON

Illustrations by Lindsay Long
Cover design by Faceout Studio, Molly von Borstel
Interior design by Janelle Coury
Cover image © Artnis, Alexander Lysenko, natrot / Shutterstock

For bulk, special sales, or ministry purchases, please call 1-800-547-8979.
Email: CustomerService@hhpbooks.com

 This logo is a federally registered trademark of the Hawkins Children's LLC. Harvest House Publishers, Inc., is the exclusive licensee of this trademark.

M Is for Mama Study Guide

Copyright © 2024 by Abbie Halberstadt
Published by Harvest House Publishers
Eugene, Oregon 97408
www.harvesthousepublishers.com

ISBN 978-0-7369-9099-8 (pbk)

Printed in the United States of America

24 25 26 27 28 29 30 31 32 / KP / 10 9 8 7 6 5 4 3 2 1

Contents

Introduction

Friend, I'm so glad you're here, and I can't wait to link arms with you in the sisterhood of rebellion against mediocre motherhood. The thing is, we *all* struggle with mediocrity (whether it's moments, days, or years) without Christ's work at power within us. But *praise God* He walks with us through each meltdown moment, each first-trimester fog of exhaustion, each carelessly spoken word—never condemning, always spurring us onward and upward in His strength.

In this *M Is for Mama Study Guide*, you'll receive practical, nitty-gritty, thought-provoking content in each chapter to help you glean more from the book and to really sink your teeth into what it means to live counterculturally in a time when it would be so much easier (not to mention celebrated!) to go with society's flow.

I've broken down each chapter into a series of key-point summaries, action steps, questions for reflection, and even a guided prayer.

You'll also have room to respond to prompts and journal a few things for each topic. And I've provided a QR code for access to accompanying video content from me for each chapter. This is the ideal companion to *M Is for Mama* (or MIFM for short) for gleaning maximum impact on an individual level.

Video Link

However, I've also included discussion questions, which makes this guide the perfect tool to help you band together with kindred mamas who are also seeking to buck trends of apathy and resentment in motherhood. I have been so blessed to receive dozens of messages from mamas who have hosted MIFM book clubs (even before this study guide came out!) and who still meet with the mamas from their group. *M Is for Mama* has been the catalyst that helped them break through shyness or past rejection to find their "mama tribe"—a true "iron sharpening iron" band of sisters! (I've even been privileged to meet whole MIFM groups when they road-tripped to attend a book signing or other event—a huge thrill!)

Whether this guide serves you individually or collectively, I pray it enriches your experience with *M Is for Mama*—and that God uses it to draw you closer to Him and higher toward His calling for you as a mama.

The Culture of Mediocre Motherhood

EXAMINING THE ATTITUDES THAT KEEP US FROM CHRISTLIKE EXCELLENCE

The first chapter explores the attitudes that keep mamas stuck in a cycle of mediocrity—our current culture's standard—as opposed to striving for a Christlike view of motherhood. For mamas to be willing to choose to follow Christ's model for motherhood, they must first be able to see how the current culture is dragging them down into self-pity and complacency. Most importantly, they need to see the benefits of the Christlike model. Applying biblical wisdom to motherhood doesn't mean our lives will be a cakewalk. But it does mean we will be mothering "as unto the Lord," which brings the peace of knowing we are following in Christ's example—a practice that produces fruit in not only us but our children as well. That is a powerful incentive!

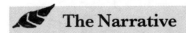 **The Narrative**

Read the examples of mediocre motherhood and Christlike motherhood in your book. Take some time to pray about the areas in which you might be embracing mediocre motherhood and record them here. Then reflect on what those same issues might look like through a lens of Christlike motherhood.

MEDIOCRE MOTHERHOOD	CHRISTLIKE MOTHERHOOD

Action Steps

Memorize and meditate on Proverbs 11:14 (ESV): "Where there is no guidance, a people falls, but in an abundance of counselors there is safety." One helpful way to memorize Scripture is to start by writing it down.

Make a list of three Christlike mamas whom you could seek out for help and guidance.

1. ....

2. ....

3. ....

Unfollow accounts that glorify and glamorize snark, hopelessness, or abdication of responsibility in motherhood. What kinds of accounts did you unfollow?

....

....

....

....

....

....

Reflection Questions

Am I using Scripture as my standard for excellence in motherhood?

....

....

....

....

....

....

Do I feel validated when I see others struggling (and failing) in the same areas as I am?

Am I willing to make changes to my attitudes and behavior when the Holy Spirit convicts me?

IT IS God WHO WORKS IN YOU.

PHILIPPIANS 2:13

Group Discussion Questions

Video Link

Up to this point, what has been your definition of "being a good mama"?

_____

_____

_____

_____

_____

_____

_____

What have you heard, seen, or read lately that strikes you as an example of mediocre motherhood disguised as relatability? What is the lie hiding behind the example you chose?

_____

_____

_____

_____

_____

_____

_____

_____

_____

In what area of motherhood do you struggle most to not compare yourself unfavorably to other moms?

Apart from Christ, we are all going to struggle with mediocrity. How does that realization change the way you see your own shortcomings as a mama?

How can our weaknesses help us conform to the image of Christ?

_____

_____

_____

_____

_____

_____

_____

Prayer

Lord, thank You for giving wisdom generously and without reproach to all who ask (James 1:5). May we turn to You each day in every area of our lives, including motherhood, recognizing that conformity to Christ is infinitely better than fitting in with the world.

No Two Good Mamas Look Alike

KICKING COMPARISON AND EMBRACING OUR GIFTINGS IN CHRIST

This chapter encourages mamas to celebrate each other's uniqueness and avoid falling into the traps of comparison and competition that lead to discouragement and isolation. When we understand that God gave each of us different strengths and weaknesses, not only does this free us up to experience the joy of camaraderie with other mamas but it also helps us see how He created us to serve and be served by others. We feel so much more capable of Christlike motherhood when we have a support system of other mamas to share in our journey.

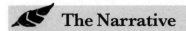

The Narrative

Read the examples of mediocre motherhood and Christlike motherhood in your book. Take some time to pray about the areas in which you might be embracing mediocre motherhood and record them here. Then reflect on what those same issues might look like through a lens of Christlike motherhood.

MEDIOCRE MOTHERHOOD	CHRISTLIKE MOTHERHOOD

Action Steps

Write out, memorize, and meditate on 2 Corinthians 10:12 (ESV): "Not that we dare to classify or compare ourselves with some of those who are commending themselves. But when they measure themselves by one another and compare themselves with one another, they are without understanding."

Make a list of three things the Lord has given you the ability to do well and three things you struggle with.

Things I do well:

1. ....
....
....

2. ....
....
....

3. ....
....
....

My areas of struggle:

1. ....
....
....

2. ....
....
....

3. ....
....
....

Choose one thing you can do this week to exercise a particular gifting and one thing you can do to strengthen an area in which you are weak.

_____

_____

_____

_____

_____

_____

_____

_____

Reflection Questions

Am I avoiding community because I'm afraid I won't measure up?

_____

_____

_____

_____

_____

_____

_____

Do I tend to look down on others who aren't "performing" as well as I am?

Am I using my giftings to bless my children and others?

WHETHER YOU **EAT** OR **DRINK** OR WHATEVER YOU DO, DO IT ALL FOR THE **GLORY** OF **GOD.**

1 CORINTHIANS 10:31

Group Discussion Questions

Video Link

What impact has social media had on your relationships with other mamas? Has it brought you closer or divided you?

_____

_____

_____

_____

_____

_____

_____

What comes easily for you as a mama? How could you use this area of strength to bless other mamas?

_____

_____

_____

_____

_____

_____

_____

_____

When does an area of weakness become sin?

_____

_____

_____

_____

_____

_____

What is an area in which you hear the Holy Spirit whispering, "Do better"?

_____

_____

_____

_____

_____

_____

_____

_____

What are the differences between saying, "No two mamas are created alike" and, "There is no right or wrong way to do motherhood"?

Prayer

Lord, You say in Your Word that those who compare and measure themselves by others for their worth are not wise (2 Corinthians 10:12). Please help us to be grateful for the things You've made us good at and willing to work on the areas in which we struggle.

What Is That to You? Follow Me

STAYING THE COURSE REGARDLESS OF WHAT ANYONE ELSE IS DOING

There is a seemingly endless supply of advice available to mamas, some of which is well-intentioned but often confusing or conflicting with biblical truth. How do we sift through the myriad dos and don'ts of motherhood to incorporate the good ideas and reject the harmful ones? This chapter encourages and challenges mamas to filter what they see and hear about motherhood through the truth of Scripture, building their discernment and becoming more confident in their identity in Christ.

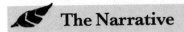 **The Narrative**

Read the examples of mediocre motherhood and Christlike motherhood in your book. Take some time to pray about the areas in which you might be embracing mediocre motherhood and record them here. Then reflect on what those same issues might look like through a lens of Christlike motherhood.

MEDIOCRE MOTHERHOOD	CHRISTLIKE MOTHERHOOD

Action Steps

Write out, memorize, and meditate on Galatians 1:10 (ESV): "For am I now seeking the approval of man, or of God? Or am I trying to please man? If I were still trying to please man, I would not be a servant of Christ."

Talk to your kids about what it looks like to follow Jesus even when no one else is. Take note of the areas in which you struggle with this.

_____

_____

_____

_____

_____

_____

_____

_____

Make a list of the top five influences you can identify.

1. _____

2. _____

3. _____

4. _____

5. _____

Reflection Questions

Do I look to friends or social media for validation, or do I consult the Bible first?

Am I swayed by how my culture says I should mother, even if it flies in the face of Scripture?

Am I teaching truth and godly conviction to my children and then practicing it consistently?

_____

_____

_____

_____

_____

_____

_____

Group Discussion Questions

What is the best advice you've ever received as a mom? Who gave you this advice?

Video Link

_____

_____

_____

_____

_____

_____

_____

What are some questions or comments from other mamas that bother you?
Why?

How can we handle questions that aren't specifically addressed in Scripture?

What does "staying in your lane" as a Christian mama mean to you?

What is an area in which you overthink what others are doing? What does the Bible say about this issue?

_____

_____

_____

_____

_____

_____

_____

_____

_____

_____

_____

_____

_____

_____

Prayer

Lord, as servants of Christ, we don't want anything that anybody else does to take our eyes off of You. Increase our affections for You and our children each day as we "press on toward the goal to win the prize for which God has called [us] heavenward in Christ Jesus" (Philippians 3:14).

And What Does the Lord Require of Thee?

SURRENDERING OUR VERSION OF PERFECT MOTHERHOOD TO HIS PERFECT WILL

Now that we've established that God is the only right source of understanding for our roles as mamas, what is He asking us to do, and how do we do it? Fortunately, God has spelled it out for us in His Word. This doesn't mean that doing what He requires from us will be easy—far from it at times—but there is hope. We are not alone in our pursuit of Christlikeness. We have each other and, more importantly, God will meet us in the weak moments when we reach out to Him.

🖋 The Narrative

Read the examples of mediocre motherhood and Christlike motherhood in your book. Take some time to pray about the areas in which you might be embracing mediocre motherhood and record them here. Then reflect on what those same issues might look like through a lens of Christlike motherhood.

MEDIOCRE MOTHERHOOD	CHRISTLIKE MOTHERHOOD

🌿 Action Steps

Write out, memorize, and meditate on Proverbs 3:5-6 (ESV): "Trust in the LORD with all your heart, and do not lean on your own understanding. In all your ways acknowledge Him, and He will make straight your paths."

Identify areas in motherhood that feel scary to you and ask the Lord to help you trust His will in them.

Pick one exercise of "trusting the Lord" to do with your kids this week. Write out your intention here, as a way to commit to the exercise.

Reflection Questions

Do I really believe that God's plans for me are better than mine?

_____

_____

_____

_____

_____

_____

_____

Am I willing to do hard or scary things even when the world tells me I would be foolish to do so?

_____

_____

_____

_____

_____

_____

_____

_____

_____

Do JUSTLY Love MERCY AND Walk HUMBLY WITH YOUR GOD

MICAH 6:8

Am I modeling trust in Christ to my children on a daily basis?

Group Discussion Questions

How is God revealing His calling to you?

Video Link

What is keeping you from praying, "Lord, show me what You have for me and then equip me to do it by Your power, even if it's nothing like I imagined it would be"?

When have you felt unfairly burdened? When have you felt undeservedly blessed by God? What do these experiences have in common?

How do you balance doing for others with meeting your own physical, emotional, and spiritual needs?

_____

_____

_____

_____

Are you wrestling with a particular issue for which you truly don't know the right (godly) answer? If so, what is it?

_____

_____

_____

_____

_____

_____

_____

_____

Prayer

*Lord, we know that every good and perfect gift comes from You
(James 1:17), and we desire to recognize Your goodness in every
aspect of our lives. Open our eyes to the ways that You are directing
our paths in motherhood so that we can walk boldly in Your will.*

5

Self-Care Versus Soul Care

RECOGNIZING THAT TIME WITH CHRIST IS BETTER THAN "ME TIME"

Self-care has become a modern-day Trojan horse, bringing with it a whole host of attitudes and actions that can lead us away from our missions as Christ-seeking mamas. We'll explore how to walk that precarious tightrope of caring for ourselves physically and spiritually without becoming overly self-indulgent or unnecessarily denying ourselves rest and refreshment. Looking to Jesus as our example, we can achieve the balance that allows us to care for ourselves so that we can properly care for others.

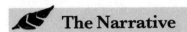 **The Narrative**

Read the examples of mediocre motherhood and Christlike motherhood in your book. Take some time to pray about the areas in which you might be embracing mediocre motherhood and record them here. Then reflect on what those same issues might look like through a lens of Christlike motherhood.

MEDIOCRE MOTHERHOOD	CHRISTLIKE MOTHERHOOD

Action Steps

Write out, memorize, and meditate on Philippians 4:19 (ESV): "And my God will supply every need of yours according to his riches in glory in Christ Jesus."

Commit to spending time in the soul care of prayer and reading God's Word three times this week. Record what you read and when you prayed.

☐ ....

☐ ....

☐ ....

Choose and do one self-care activity (a shower, a workout, ten pages of a good book...) that brings joy and helps you to serve your family better. What will it be?

....

....

....

....

....

....

....

Reflection Questions

Am I using self-care as an excuse for self-indulgence?

....

....

....

....

....

....

Conversely, am I denying myself basic needs in the name of "taking up my cross," even though it's detrimental to my health and makes me a less effective mother?

_____

_____

_____

_____

_____

_____

How can my kids and I choose soul care together this week?

_____

_____

_____

_____

_____

_____

_____

_____

_____

AND MY
GOD
WILL
SUPPLY
all
your
needs
PHILIPPIANS 4:19 CSB

Group Discussion Questions

What is your idea of the perfect five-minute break?
How does it help you recharge?

Video Link

_____

_____

_____

_____

_____

_____

_____

_____

How do you react when your quiet time is encroached upon?

_____

_____

_____

_____

_____

_____

_____

What is one thing that you've been denying yourself? Is there a good reason for this?

_____

_____

_____

_____

_____

_____

_____

How do you view your time spent with God? Does it feel rejuvenating or more like a chore?

_____

_____

_____

_____

_____

_____

_____

What steps can you take to avoid burnout?

_____

_____

_____

_____

_____

_____

_____

_____

_____

_____

_____

_____

_____

Prayer

*Lord, You already know what we need before we ask (Matthew
6:8), but You still desire that we come to You to be filled
with Your presence. Keep us focused on caring for our souls
with Your Word and prayer, trusting that You will supply
everything else we need because You love us so well.*

When We're Guilty of Mom Guilt

LEARNING THE DIFFERENCE BETWEEN SHAME AND HOLY SPIRIT CONVICTION

We all experience mom guilt at different times. The key to not getting trapped in a place of continuous condemnation lies in having a proper understanding of the difference between fleshly guilt and Holy Spirit–initiated conviction. We can also learn to seek God's help to accomplish what needs to be done and spend less time beating ourselves up for the things we weren't able to do in our own power. Staying mired in guilt gives the enemy an open door to speak lies into our hearts that fly in the face of the truth of our identities in Christ. This chapter encourages and reminds us to stay grounded in God's Word so that guilt does not grow into a full-on shame spiral.

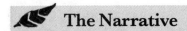 **The Narrative**

Read the examples of mediocre motherhood and Christlike motherhood in your book. Take some time to pray about the areas in which you might be embracing mediocre motherhood and record them here. Then reflect on what those same issues might look like through a lens of Christlike motherhood.

MEDIOCRE MOTHERHOOD	CHRISTLIKE MOTHERHOOD

Action Steps

Write out, memorize, and meditate on Romans 8:1 (ESV): "There is therefore now no condemnation for those who are in Christ Jesus."

Make a list of three lies Satan wants you to believe about your mothering, and then find the truth in Scripture.

1. Lie: _____

Truth: _____

_____

_____

2. Lie: _____

Truth: _____

_____

_____

3. Lie: _____

Truth: _____

_____

_____

Ask the Lord to reveal one area of genuine Holy Spirit conviction and how to address it.

_____

_____

_____

_____

_____

_____

_____

AS FAR AS THE EAST IS FROM THE WEST

PSALM 103:12

Reflection Questions

Am I allowing false mom guilt to keep me trapped in condemnation?

On the other hand, am I ignoring areas that need to be addressed because I'm believing the world's "perfect just the way you are" mantra?

What is one way I can model being in tune with the Holy Spirit this week to my children?

_____

_____

_____

_____

_____

_____

_____

Group Discussion Questions

What is your reaction at the end of the day if you haven't checked everything off your to-do list?

Video Link

_____

_____

_____

_____

_____

_____

_____

_____

As you consider things that make you feel guilty, are these areas you can control? If not, does that change how you view them?

_____

_____

_____

_____

_____

_____

_____

How do you typically deal with guilt?

_____

_____

_____

_____

_____

_____

_____

_____

How could your "guilt" (conviction) sometimes be a good thing?

_____

_____

_____

_____

Does the realization that you are not captain of your own ship comfort or concern you?

_____

_____

_____

_____

_____

_____

_____

Prayer

Lord, You have separated our sins from us as far as the east is from the west (Psalm 103:12), and You are gracious to convict us when our mothering doesn't look like what Scripture teaches. Strengthen our wills to resist Satan's lies of condemnation, and soften our hearts to accept the Holy Spirit's nudges of conviction.

The Profession of Motherhood

EMBRACING OUR PRIMARY CALLING IN THE FACE OF CULTURAL DISDAIN

With so many lucrative at-home businesses and side hustles available to moms today, there is more pressure than ever to "balance" raising children with other pursuits. Though there is nothing inherently wrong with the desire to work and earn money, we can lose sight of our God-given responsibilities as parents if this becomes our primary focus. On top of that, sometimes we don't hold ourselves to the same professional standards at home as we would in the workplace. When we see motherhood as our most important job and not just as an obligation—or worse yet, an obstacle to overcome—we can experience the peace and joy that come with being in line with God's priorities for our lives. Not only that, but our children thrive when their mama recognizes that raising and discipling them is a high and holy calling.

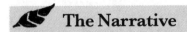 **The Narrative**

Read the examples of mediocre motherhood and Christlike motherhood in your book. Take some time to pray about the areas in which you might be embracing mediocre motherhood and record them here. Then reflect on what those same issues might look like through a lens of Christlike motherhood.

MEDIOCRE MOTHERHOOD	CHRISTLIKE MOTHERHOOD

Action Steps

Write out, memorize, and meditate on Colossians 3:23-24 (ESV): "Whatever you do, work heartily, as for the Lord and not for men, knowing that from the Lord you will receive the inheritance as your reward. You are serving the Lord Christ."

List five things that you can do to improve professionally as a mother, and then pick one to focus on this week.

1. ....

....

2. ....

....

3. ....

....

4. ....

....

5. ....

....

Ask your kids for ways that you can serve them better (be prepared to be humbled!).

....

....

....

....

....

....

....

....

YOU ARE SERVING THE **LORD CHRIST**

COLOSSIANS 3:24 ESV

Reflection Questions

Do I truly approach motherhood as a profession at which to excel every day?

_____

_____

_____

_____

_____

_____

Am I more excited by the concept of having my kids "out of my hair" or by the prospect of raising up eternal souls for Christ's kingdom?

_____

_____

_____

_____

_____

_____

_____

_____

_____

_____

Do I believe that I, first and foremost, have been tasked with the primary privilege of training up my kids to love God?

_____

_____

_____

_____

_____

_____

_____

_____

Group Discussion Questions

If you have a profession or side job, how do you currently balance that with motherhood? Has reading this chapter changed your perspective on that balance?

Video Link

_____

_____

_____

_____

_____

How do you feel about the phrase "the profession of motherhood"?

How would you rate your job satisfaction as a mom? What is currently missing for you to feel more fulfilled in your role?

Has being a mom been a difficult adjustment for you? If so, how?

_____

_____

_____

_____

_____

What messages are you sending your children by how you approach your job as a mom?

_____

_____

_____

_____

_____

_____

_____

_____

_____

_____

Prayer

Lord, You know that we grow weary of the ceaselessness of the profession of motherhood. Help us to truly recognize its worth in a culture that values it little. Help us to do even the little things "as for You," knowing that we are serving Christ and our children in the process.

8

When the Seat of Our Pants Tears

LEARNING THE ART OF SELF-DISCIPLINE

Training children in the way they should go is one of the most important responsibilities a mama has, but it can also be one of the most intimidating, especially if our background has not equipped us well for the task. Before we can expect to see our efforts bear fruit in our children, we must first commit to training ourselves. After all, we don't want to be hypocrites—requiring something of our children that we ourselves avoid at all costs. With God's help, we can be consistent! But we need to develop discipline to study His Word and pray consistently so we can stay connected to Him and understand the precepts we will use to "train up" our children. This will be a tough chapter for many moms, but the good news is that God already knows our struggles and inadequacies and offers us grace upon grace in our areas of weakness. Our job is to commit each day to Him so that we can experience His guidance and care.

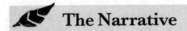 **The Narrative**

Read the examples of mediocre motherhood and Christlike motherhood in your book. Take some time to pray about the areas in which you might be embracing mediocre motherhood and record them here. Then reflect on what those same issues might look like through a lens of Christlike motherhood.

MEDIOCRE MOTHERHOOD	CHRISTLIKE MOTHERHOOD

Action Steps

Write out, memorize, and meditate on 2 Timothy 3:16 (esv): "All Scripture is breathed out by God and profitable for teaching, for reproof, for correction, and for training in righteousness."

_____

_____

_____

_____

_____

Identify three areas in which you lack discipline; choose one to focus on this week.

1. ....

2. ....

3. ....

My focus this week:

....

....

....

Make a plan to incorporate regular Scripture reading (we love *The One Year Bible*) and memorization into your routine. How will you make it happen?

....

....

....

....

....

....

....

....

....

....

....

....

Reflection Questions

How can I be more consistent to do the "needful things" that draw me close to God and help my household run more smoothly?

_____

_____

_____

_____

_____

_____

Am I disciplined in some areas but lack fortitude when it comes to studying God's Word? Why?

_____

_____

_____

_____

_____

_____

_____

_____

_____

HE *gently*
LEADS THOSE
THAT HAVE
young

ISAIAH 40:11

If I am facing overwhelm, how much of that is a result of my own lack of self-training?

_____

_____

_____

_____

_____

_____

_____

Group Discussion Questions

Of the four questions posed on page 106 of *M Is for Mama* ("A Biblical Gut Check"), which is the most challenging for you?

Video Link

_____

_____

_____

_____

_____

_____

_____

In what area(s) do you need more training and discipline in order to model Christlike behavior to your children?

_____

_____

_____

_____

_____

_____

How do you handle disappointment when you don't see progress?

_____

_____

_____

_____

_____

_____

_____

_____

_____

_____

What kind of upbringing did you have, and how do you think that has aided or detracted from your ability to be self-disciplined?

_____

_____

_____

_____

_____

How can accountability with this group help set you on a right path of correcting bad habits and establishing godly ones?

_____

_____

_____

_____

_____

_____

_____

_____

_____

Prayer

Lord, You gave us the perfect example of discipline in Jesus, who was "obedient to death—even death on a cross" (Philippians 2:8). May we emulate His example, knowing that whatever discomfort we experience in the self-training process will ultimately produce great fruit.

The Gentleness Challenge

PRACTICAL HOPE
FOR ANGRY MOMS

As women and moms, we have a plethora of seemingly legitimate excuses for getting frustrated, angry, and disillusioned while raising children and managing our households. The culture of mediocre motherhood revels in these excuses, wallowing in the hard and sharing empty platitudes that we are all human and "in this together." This chapter challenges Christian mamas to examine their own reactions to the stressors of motherhood in the light of God's truth. Though we can acknowledge the hard, we also need to take action to ensure we don't get stuck in a cycle of disappointment and discouragement that robs us and our families of the freedom that Christ won for us on the cross.

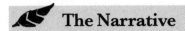 ## The Narrative

Read the examples of mediocre motherhood and Christlike motherhood in your book. Take some time to pray about the areas in which you might be embracing mediocre motherhood and record them here. Then reflect on what those same issues might look like through a lens of Christlike motherhood.

MEDIOCRE MOTHERHOOD	CHRISTLIKE MOTHERHOOD

Action Steps

Write out, memorize, and meditate on Ephesians 4:2 (ESV): "Be completely humble and gentle; be patient, bearing with one another in love."

Sit down and identify symptoms of hormonal overwhelm.

_____

_____

_____

_____

_____

Outline three practical steps (such as the Gentleness Challenge, eating snacks regularly, taking fifteen-minute power naps, or unfollowing off-base social media accounts) to overcome the urges to take out bad days on your family.

1. _____

_____

2. _____

_____

3. _____

_____

Reflection Questions

In what ways am I "completely humble and gentle"? In what ways am I not?

_____

_____

_____

_____

_____

_____

If I were to ask my kids to describe my speech, what would they say?

_____

_____

_____

_____

_____

_____

_____

_____

How can I invite my whole family into my efforts to use gentle speech?

_____

_____

_____

_____

_____

_____

_____

_____

_____

_____

GRACIOUS WORDS ARE LIKE A HONEYCOMB

PROVERBS 16:24 ESV

Group Discussion Questions

Video Link

On a scale of 1 to 10, where is your "offendometer" right now? How do you respond when your emotions are high?

_____

_____

_____

_____

_____

_____

_____

After reading this chapter, has your view changed regarding how our culture discusses the trials of motherhood? If so, how?

_____

_____

_____

_____

_____

_____

_____

_____

_____

_____

What would be your biggest challenge in speaking gently to your family for thirty days?

_____

_____

_____

_____

_____

_____

_____

Are feelings a true indicator of who we really are? How much weight do you give your emotions?

_____

_____

_____

_____

_____

_____

_____

_____

_____

_____

Outside of hormones, what can trigger your emotions as a mom?

_____

_____

_____

_____

_____

_____

_____

_____

_____

_____

Prayer

Lord, You are so patient with us, slow to anger and abounding in love (Numbers 14:18). Teach us to follow Your example and check our rough, impatient speech at the door of our mouths.

Training Our Kids in the Way They Should Go

FOUR PRINCIPLES FOR INSTILLING GOOD HABITS

Despite what culture tells us, children absolutely need training—not because they are like animals but because they, like every other human, will be quick to do what is "right in their own eyes" if we do not guide them toward biblical truth. If we choose not to take on this very necessary task, we are doing our children a huge disservice, not to mention disobeying God. Instilling biblical precepts in our children from a very early age isn't easy and will be frustrating at times. But doing the hard work now will pay huge dividends as our children grow and mature—for us, for our kids, and for the world at large!

🖋 The Narrative

Read the examples of mediocre motherhood and Christlike motherhood in your book. Take some time to pray about the areas in which you might be embracing mediocre motherhood and record them here. Then reflect on what those same issues might look like through a lens of Christlike motherhood.

MEDIOCRE MOTHERHOOD	CHRISTLIKE MOTHERHOOD

🌱 Action Steps

Write out, memorize, and meditate on Hebrews 12:11 (ESV): "For the moment all discipline seems painful rather than pleasant, but later it yields the peaceful fruit of righteousness to those who have been trained by it."

Choose three things that will help you practically with staying consistent in training your kids. (My favorites are alarms as reminders to do something, timers to stay on track, and simple prep like laying out shoes and snacks before leaving the house.)

1. _____

_____

2. _____

_____

3. _____

_____

Place scriptural affirmations of the benefits of training around your home as motivation to keep going. Record some of those affirmations here.

_____

_____

_____

_____

_____

_____

_____

_____

_____

_____

_____

_____

YOU
SHALL TEACH
THEM
DILIGENTLY
TO
YOUR CHILDREN

DEUTERONOMY 6:7 BSB

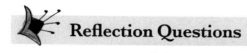

Reflection Questions

In what ways am I embracing my God-given position as "mama" rather than "best bud"? In what ways am I not?

What keeps me from being consistent or following through? How can I tweak those things?

Do I truly believe that training up my children in the way they should go will make a significant difference in their lives? If so, how am I exemplifying that?

_____

_____

_____

_____

_____

_____

_____

Group Discussion Questions

What does being a truth-teller to your children look like for you?

Video Link

_____

_____

_____

_____

_____

_____

_____

What would help you become more consistent with follow-through on disciplining your children?

_____

_____

_____

_____

_____

_____

_____

What would be your biggest challenge in speaking gently to your family for thirty days?

_____

_____

_____

_____

_____

_____

_____

_____

_____

How can you mirror God's faithful character to your kids? What changes would you need to make to achieve that?

_____

_____

_____

_____

_____

When is it okay to "let things slide"? In what areas are you too lenient with your children? Or too strict?

_____

_____

_____

_____

_____

_____

_____

_____

_____

Prayer

Lord, You never give up on us, no matter how stubborn or intractable we are. And we know You love us because You discipline us (Hebrews 12:6). Help us to follow Your example by loving our children well enough to train them in Your ways.

The Penny Reward System

A SIMPLE WAY TO ENCOURAGE GOOD CHOICES

If your children (like many) have a difficult time recognizing that righteousness is its own reward, this simple system can be an effective way of noticing and celebrating right choices. I always encourage moms to customize the PRS to fit their family's needs or come up with their own system, but if you need extra guidance, I also wrote an e-book to answer all of the detailed questions (you can find it at misformama.net/penny-reward -system). The point is not a rote "performance + reward" model but instead an encouragement to pay attention so that we can genuinely "catch" our children doing something especially kind or helpful and then unexpectedly and delightedly encourage and uplift them to "not grow weary of doing good" (Galatians 6:9 ESV).

The Narrative

Read the examples of mediocre motherhood and Christlike motherhood in your book. Take some time to pray about the areas in which you might be embracing mediocre motherhood and record them here. Then reflect on what those same issues might look like through a lens of Christlike motherhood.

MEDIOCRE MOTHERHOOD	CHRISTLIKE MOTHERHOOD

Action Steps

Write out, memorize, and meditate on Matthew 25:29 (ESV): "For to everyone who has will more be given, and he will have an abundance. But from the one who has not, even what he has will be taken away."

Consider what "talents" the Lord has given you and whether you are stewarding them well for His glory.

_____

_____

_____

_____

_____

_____

Choose a practical method to increase the peace in your home. Consider implementing the PRS or something similar as a way of encouraging and reminding your kids to choose wisely. What kind of system would be a good fit for your family?

_____

_____

_____

_____

_____

_____

_____

_____

_____

WELL DONE GOOD AND FAITHFUL SERVANT

MATTHEW 25:23

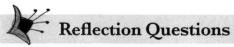 **Reflection Questions**

Have I taken measures to create a peaceful atmosphere in our home, or am I flying by the seat of my pants?

Do I let comparison to others' methods paralyze my attempts to establish helpful systems in my home?

What are my strengths and weaknesses in this area? How can I improve?

_____

_____

_____

_____

_____

_____

_____

Group Discussion Questions

What methods of encouragement do your children respond best to? How could these be incorporated in your system?

Video Link

_____

_____

_____

_____

_____

_____

How do you feel about encouraging good habits with external motivation? Do we see anywhere in the Bible that God blesses His children with good things when they do right?

_____

_____

_____

_____

_____

_____

_____

What systems have you tried before? What worked and what didn't?

_____

_____

_____

_____

_____

_____

_____

_____

_____

What part of teaching your children to love and do the right thing is most difficult for you?

_____

_____

_____

_____

_____

_____

In what ways do your kids show kindness?

_____

_____

_____

_____

_____

_____

Prayer

Lord, in the parable of the talents, You teach us to take the resources we've been given and multiply them for Your kingdom. May we be willing to make the effort of finding out what works best to bring peace and order to our families so that we can glorify You.

Boot Camp Parenting

CORRECTING BIG BAD HABITS WITH A BITE-SIZED APPROACH

Though the name may sound drastic, "boot camp parenting" is really just a way of focusing concentrated effort on one problem area at a time. It's often tempting, and frankly easier (at least in the short term), to hope our children will just grow out of unhelpful behaviors rather than try to work through the issues. Or maybe it all seems so overwhelming that we don't know where to start. By breaking behavioral challenges down into smaller components and devoting one focused week to addressing a specific area, we can alleviate the strain of letting the problem persist and causing ourselves and our kids more problems and stress in the long run. Being willing to tackle minor frustrations *now* before they grow into big bad habits is just one small way we can faithfully run the race of parenting well in Christ's strength.

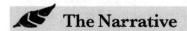 **The Narrative**

Read the examples of mediocre motherhood and Christlike motherhood in your book. Take some time to pray about the areas in which you might be embracing mediocre motherhood and record them here. Then reflect on what those same issues might look like through a lens of Christlike motherhood.

MEDIOCRE MOTHERHOOD	CHRISTLIKE MOTHERHOOD

Action Steps

Write out, memorize, and meditate on Proverbs 29:17 (ESV): "Discipline your son, and he will give you rest; he will give delight to your heart."

Take the time to evaluate hard kid situations to determine whether they are merely phases or full-blown bad habits.

Lay out specific "boot camp" parenting strategies for the areas that qualify as bad habits.

Reflection Questions

What is keeping me from addressing problem areas (fear, laziness, overwhelm, distraction…)?

What am I willing to sacrifice to help my kids overcome struggles with bad habits?

_____

_____

_____

_____

_____

_____

_____

_____

What does digging in and doing the hard work of parenting say to my kids?

_____

_____

_____

_____

_____

_____

_____

_____

FOR THE *Lord* GIVES WISDOM

PROVERBS 2:6

Group Discussion Questions

Are you in a difficult parenting phase right now? If so, how are you coping with it?

Video Link

_____

_____

_____

_____

_____

_____

_____

How could your biggest parenting dilemma be turned into bite-sized goals?

_____

_____

_____

_____

_____

_____

_____

_____

_____

If you have multiple children, how has your perspective on getting through tough phases changed over the years?

Is there a bad habit that you have let go unchecked for too long? If so, why?

Think of a parenting victory you've had in correcting a bad habit. How did you solve the issue, and how long did it take?

_____

_____

_____

_____

_____

_____

_____

_____

_____

_____

_____

_____

_____

_____

Prayer

Lord, nothing compares with the "hard" of the cross. Please make us mindful of those areas that require focused attention and give us perseverance to not "grow weary of doing good" (Galatians 6:9 ESV).

Cultivating a Peaceful Home

CONSTANT FIGHTING
DOESN'T HAVE TO
BE THE NORM

As we explore how to teach our children to live at peace with each other and others, this chapter exposes one of the biggest lies of mediocre motherhood—that "relatable" is the same thing as "acceptable." We can all relate to wanting to "get even," but this doesn't legitimize the sinful behavior. Cultivating a peaceful home requires a lot of repetitive, consistent follow-through on our part, not only by reminding our children to choose godly behaviors but also by modeling those actions ourselves. It's a lot of work! But it is *so* worth the effort in the dividends of peace and joy it pays in return.

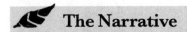 **The Narrative**

Read the examples of mediocre motherhood and Christlike motherhood in your book. Take some time to pray about the areas in which you might be embracing mediocre motherhood and record them here. Then reflect on what those same issues might look like through a lens of Christlike motherhood.

MEDIOCRE MOTHERHOOD	CHRISTLIKE MOTHERHOOD

Action Steps

Write out, memorize, and meditate on Proverbs 17:1 (ESV): "Better is a dry morsel with quiet than a house full of feasting with strife."

Call a family meeting to lay out how you will deal with sibling strife going forward. Be specific about what qualifies as "bickering" or "unkindness" in your home. What will you address?

Enact a system like the PRS that will help your kids be mindful about their speech and actions as you either reward or discipline them. How does your system work?

LIVE at PEACE
with everyone
ROMANS 12:18

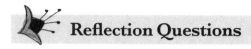

Reflection Questions

Have I fallen into the habit of believing that constant bickering is unavoidable? If so, why?

What factors have contributed when unkindness is on the uptick in my home?

How can I exemplify the truth that "we love because he first loved us"?

_____

_____

_____

_____

_____

_____

_____

_____

Group Discussion Questions

What typically starts a fight in your house? What underlying sin is causing your children to act out?

Video Link

_____

_____

_____

_____

_____

_____

_____

How do you resolve your children's disagreements? What have you seen success with?

_____

_____

_____

_____

_____

_____

_____

Has your upbringing affected how you view your children's fights? If so, how?

_____

_____

_____

_____

_____

_____

_____

_____

_____

_____

What is an area where setting expectations ahead of time would help your children?

_____

_____

_____

_____

_____

How do you model healthy conflict resolution to your children?

_____

_____

_____

_____

_____

_____

_____

Prayer

> *Lord, we are way too good at doing "whatever seem[s] right in [our] own eyes" (Judges 21:25 NLT) without regard for how it affects other people. Help us to set the example of treating others in the way we want to be treated and to truly be at peace with everyone in our families and beyond.*

We Are the Gatekeepers

BECAUSE THE MEDIA WE CONSUME MATTERS

Taking an active role in being aware of and regulating the media our children are exposed to is one of the key areas where we as Christian mamas must rise above the culture's standard that puts our kids at constant risk of isolation and exploitation. Our role as media "gatekeepers" is more crucial than ever as media drifts further and further from Christian values—or even "traditional" notions of goodness and decency (which have their roots in God's laws). Though we can't micromanage everything our kids will be exposed to, we must remain vigilant, engaged, and willing to draw lines of conviction within our own homes with regard to what we will allow our children to watch, read, look at, and listen to.

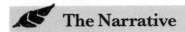 **The Narrative**

Read the examples of mediocre motherhood and Christlike motherhood in your book. Take some time to pray about the areas in which you might be embracing mediocre motherhood and record them here. Then reflect on what those same issues might look like through a lens of Christlike motherhood.

MEDIOCRE MOTHERHOOD	CHRISTLIKE MOTHERHOOD

Action Steps

Write out, memorize, and meditate on Romans 12:2 (ESV): "Do not be conformed to this world, but be transformed by the renewal of your mind, that by testing you may discern what is the will of God, what is good and acceptable and perfect."

Commit to researching any media before you allow it in your home and to discussing teachable moments. What television shows, movies, video games, or books will be on your list to review?

Make a plan for how you will prepare your kids to respond rightly to the inevitable ungodly media sources they will encounter elsewhere.

IF ANYONE
LOVES THE
WORLD,
LOVE FOR THE
FATHER
IS NOT IN THEM.

1 JOHN 2:15

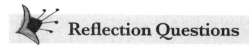 **Reflection Questions**

What are some biblical standards for media every Christian home should abide by?

Do I apply these same standards to myself as well as my children? Why or why not?

How can I be a more effective gatekeeper of my own home?

Group Discussion Questions

Where do you draw the lines in your home about what media your family consumes?

Video Link

When you look at your own media consumption, where could you use more discernment?

What are some uplifting books or television shows that your family enjoys?

When you compare the secular gold standard for children's media discussed in this chapter with God's standard, what are the biggest differences you see?

_____

_____

_____

_____

_____

_____

Do you feel pressure to allow your children to watch and read things you feel uneasy about?

_____

_____

_____

_____

_____

_____

Prayer

Lord, You say in 1 Corinthians 15:33 (ESV) that "bad company ruins good morals." Help us to be mindful of the "company" we keep in the media we allow into our homes. May we stay faithful to Your standards of truth and purity, no matter how unpopular.

The Birds and the Bees

TEACHING OUR KIDS ABOUT GOD'S GOOD DESIGN FOR SEX

Having "the talk" with our children can be intimidating, but if we don't explain God's design for sex and intimacy to them, they will form their own conclusions based on the misguided and aggressively unbiblical information they encounter at school or, gulp, from their peers. Fortunately, this task is made easier by God's Word. All we need to know and pass on about healthy sexuality can be found in the Bible, and when we emphasize God's *good* design for sex within marriage, we lay a foundation for our children's futures that includes excitement for purity and marital intimacy.

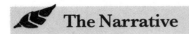 **The Narrative**

Read the examples of mediocre motherhood and Christlike motherhood in your book. Take some time to pray about the areas in which you might be embracing mediocre motherhood and record them here. Then reflect on what those same issues might look like through a lens of Christlike motherhood.

MEDIOCRE MOTHERHOOD	CHRISTLIKE MOTHERHOOD

Action Steps

Write out, memorize, and meditate on Genesis 2:24 (ESV): "Therefore a man shall leave his father and his mother and hold fast to his wife, and they shall become one flesh."

Develop a plan for talking about sex with your kids that conveys God's good plan for it. What do you want to communicate?

_____

_____

_____

_____

_____

_____

_____

_____

Take stock of technology and assess whether your kids have access to sexual information they are not ready for.

_____

_____

_____

_____

_____

_____

_____

_____

Reflection Questions

Do I have a biblical view of sex? If not, why?

_____

_____

_____

_____

_____

_____

_____

Why, when God has so clearly given it his stamp of approval inside marriage, am I so nervous to talk to my kids about sex?

_____

_____

_____

_____

_____

_____

_____

_____

_____

Honor God with your Bodies

1 CORINTHIANS 6:20

What are the benefits of my kids hearing about sex from me instead of from the world?

_____

_____

_____

_____

_____

_____

_____

Group Discussion Questions

What gives you most pause about having discussions with your children about sex and God's design for our bodies?

Video Link

_____

_____

_____

_____

_____

_____

What is your view of sex and intimacy? Is it a positive one?

How has your own upbringing and sexual history impacted how you engage with your children on this topic?

If you have already had these talks with your kids, is there anything you wish you would have said or done differently?

_____

_____

_____

_____

_____

_____

Does our current "cancel culture" climate make you hesitant to stand up for Christian values in this area?

_____

_____

_____

_____

_____

_____

_____

Prayer

Lord, You have given us the good gift of sex in marriage.
Thank you! Help us to clearly convey the joy that intimacy
with our spouse can bring and to do it boldly in a way
that combats the lies our culture seeks to spread.

16

You Don't Have to Do It All

ACCEPTING HELP IS
A GOOD IDEA

Our culture celebrates multitasking and self-sufficiency, which places incredible pressure on mamas to do it all. But does any of this line up with biblical truth? God designed us to bless and be blessed by others. He gave us Christ's church and our fellow believing brothers and sisters as support and help. For those of us who struggle to be all things to all people, our pride might be wounded by the truth that we can't do everything, but that truth should also free us. Christlike motherhood admits the need for help and freely offers it to others as well.

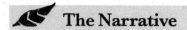 **The Narrative**

Read the examples of mediocre motherhood and Christlike motherhood in your book. Take some time to pray about the areas in which you might be embracing mediocre motherhood and record them here. Then reflect on what those same issues might look like through a lens of Christlike motherhood.

MEDIOCRE MOTHERHOOD	CHRISTLIKE MOTHERHOOD

Action Steps

Write out, memorize, and meditate on Galatians 6:2 (ESV): "Bear one another's burdens, and so fulfill the law of Christ."

Write out a list of areas in which you need help and areas in which you could offer it.

_____

_____

_____

_____

_____

_____

_____

_____

Make a plan to encourage and allow your kids to help at home in meaningful ways, even if it's inconvenient at first.

_____

_____

_____

_____

_____

_____

_____

_____

SPUR

ONE ANOTHER ON
TOWARD LOVE AND
GOOD DEEDS.

HEBREWS 10:24

Reflection Questions

Why do I sometimes feel guilty for requesting or accepting help?

_____

_____

_____

_____

_____

_____

_____

What are practical ways I can "bear another's burden" this week?

_____

_____

_____

_____

_____

_____

_____

_____

_____

How can I convey value and dignity to my children by letting them bless me
with help?

_____

_____

_____

_____

_____

_____

Group Discussion Questions

In what area do you need to ask for more help?

Video Link

_____

_____

_____

_____

_____

_____

_____

_____

_____

Do you find it easy or difficult to admit that you can't do it all?

Do you think your children are capable of helping more than they do? What keeps you from getting them more involved with chores?

How does the culture of mediocre motherhood play into the myth that we should be able to do it all?

_____

_____

_____

_____

_____

_____

_____

Do you find it uncomfortable to offer help to others? Or to accept it from them?

_____

_____

_____

_____

_____

_____

_____

Prayer

*Lord, You promise never to leave us or forsake us (Hebrews 13:5), and
yet we often act as if we must do everything on our own. Teach us to
see the deep joy in both offering help and allowing others to help us.*

17

Emotions Are Not Facts

WHY SURROUNDING OURSELVES WITH TRUTH-SPEAKERS IS ESSENTIAL TO BIBLICAL MOTHERHOOD

Emotions are extremely powerful influences on our daily lives, but they don't have to dictate our choices and actions. Praise God we have the Holy Spirit to whisper truth to our hearts, even when we are at our most sleep-deprived, hormonally imbalanced, and overwhelmed. The key is to immerse ourselves in God's Word and look to godly examples full of wisdom, rather than allowing ourselves to be swayed by nice-sounding-but-ultimately-empty platitudes like, "Your emotions are your truth" and, "All feelings are valid." Looking to Jesus and staying closely connected to others who will build us up and challenge us when needed can keep us from falling into a mire of self-pity and hopelessness, which is never where a Christian should stay.

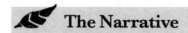 **The Narrative**

Read the examples of mediocre motherhood and Christlike motherhood in your book. Take some time to pray about the areas in which you might be embracing mediocre motherhood and record them here. Then reflect on what those same issues might look like through a lens of Christlike motherhood.

MEDIOCRE MOTHERHOOD	CHRISTLIKE MOTHERHOOD

Action Steps

Write out, memorize, and meditate on Jeremiah 17:9 (ESV): "The heart is deceitful above all things, and desperately sick; who can understand it?"

Assess the influences you allow to have a voice in your life. Are they speaking gospel truth or the empty "gospel" of feelings?

_____

_____

_____

_____

_____

_____

_____

Commit to gauging your emotions against the guide of Scripture. Journaling is a great way to do this!

_____

_____

_____

_____

_____

_____

_____

_____

Reflection Questions

How do I allow my circumstances to dictate my emotions?

Who should I be turning to for truth and encouragement in Christ?

Why are platitudes about "following your heart" ultimately empty?

_____

_____

_____

_____

_____

_____

_____

Group Discussion Questions

In what areas do you find it most difficult not to be swayed by your emotions?

Video Link

_____

_____

_____

_____

_____

_____

How does your interaction with social media affect your emotions?

_____

_____

_____

_____

_____

_____

_____

_____

Where do you go for help when your emotions are overwhelming you?

_____

_____

_____

_____

_____

_____

_____

_____

_____

_____

Therefore,
if anyone is in Christ,
he is a new Creation.

2 CORINTHIANS 5:17 ESV

Do you trust your feelings? How do you react to the cultural belief that "all feelings are valid"?

_____

_____

_____

_____

_____

_____

How can you give thanks in all circumstances?

_____

_____

_____

_____

_____

_____

_____

Prayer

Lord, we know that You experienced the full range of human emotions in Your time on this earth. And yet You did not sin. Help us to follow Your example as we bring our emotions under the Lordship of Jesus Christ and surround ourselves with godly sisters who will do the same.

Conclusion

Phew! We made it. And what a Scripture-drenched journey it was! My prayer for you throughout this process is that the Lord would speak clearly to your heart about the specific ways in which He is nudging you toward biblical excellence as a mother. As I've pointed out throughout *M Is for Mama*, the goal is conformity to no influence other than that of our Savior.

May you take the conviction and encouragement we all inevitably experience when our hearts are poised toward God and His holy Word and continue to run the race well. I can't emphasize enough how important accountability and fellowship are with staying the course in this motherhood gig. If you've been spurred on to love and good deeds (Hebrews 10:24) by an individual study guide experience, I highly encourage you to consider inviting a few friends to join with you to do it again.

Video Link

"Now may the Lord of peace himself give you peace at all times and in every way. The Lord be with all of you" (2 Thessalonians 3:16).

Organizing a Six- or Eight-Week Study

Below, you'll find suggestions for how to break the book's chapters up for a six- or eight-week study. Of course, you can do what works best for the group.

Six-week study

Week 1—intro, chapters 1 and 2
Week 2—3, 4, 5
Week 3—6, 7, 8
Week 4—9, 10, 11
Week 5—12, 13, 14
Week 6—15, 16, 17

Eight-week study

Week 1—intro, chapters 1 and 2
Week 2—3, 4
Week 3—5, 6
Week 4—7, 8
Week 5—9, 10
Week 6—11, 12
Week 7—13, 14
Week 8—15, 16, 17

Group Study Guidelines for Busy Mamas

PLAN BEFOREHAND

Before you announce the study and start inviting other mamas to join you, you'll want to determine some basic parameters. This ensures that you will be able to fulfill your role as leader without feeling frazzled in the process.

Here are some items you will want to decide prior to announcing the study:

1. **Where are we meeting?** Whether at your church, your home, a local coffee shop, or a restaurant, it is key to select a location that's convenient for you and offers enough room for the group you invite. If you plan to meet in a public area, one factor to consider is privacy. Will mamas be hesitant to share in a place their friends and neighbors frequent? This may not be an issue, but it's something to think about.

   A virtual study is also a great option (I've seen huge success with these!), but keep in mind the potential hiccups that come with online meetings—tech issues, background noise, not to mention the disconnect that comes with not being physically present as a group. Don't underestimate the value of a hug from another mama who understands what you're going through.

2. **When will we be meeting?** This is a huge issue for mamas. The main thing to ensure is that the time you choose works for you. If you're struggling to keep the time you committed to, leading the group will become an unwelcome chore, or worse yet, you'll want to quit it altogether. No time you choose will be convenient for all the mamas you invite, so don't feel guilty if one or two bow out because it doesn't fit their schedule.

   Knowing if most of the mamas in your group work or are stay-at-home or homeschool moms might make a difference, but don't assume just because a mama stays at home and her children are at school that she can drop everything and attend a midday study. Determine the best time for you and your family, and trust that God will bring the mamas to the study who need to hear the book's message. No regrets.

3. **Who will be in my group?** Determining what mamas you'll recruit to join your study might make a big difference in deciding the other details. Will you be inviting moms from your church? Your neighborhood? Your network of friends? If from church, consider putting a cap on the number of people who can sign up for the study, or make sure you have a meeting space that can accommodate a bigger group.

4. **Will childcare be available?** Because this is a book for mamas, you can't plan a study without considering the kiddos! Though it's perfectly fine to meet somewhere and not bring the children (especially if you're meeting at a coffee shop or restaurant), you will get a better turnout (and be more inclusive of single mamas) if members know they can bring their kiddos, and someone trustworthy is there to watch them. If you're meeting at church, is

there a church member or youth group worker available to help? If at home, is there a responsible older sibling looking to make a few extra bucks? Also, don't rule out dads. Many hubbies would be thrilled to help with this! Last, consider "embracing the chaos" and meeting in a kid-friendly place where the little ones can roam close by and play while you meet and talk. Moms are fantastic multitaskers, and many successful MIFM studies (with kids!) have already taken place at a local park or play place, or even in someone's backyard.

5. **How long will the study last? And how long will we meet each week?** Again, this might come down to what works best for you. Ideally, you could read a chapter per week and give yourself plenty of time to digest the content, but that's not going to be possible for most groups, which is why I've included plans for six- and eight-week studies.

   If you choose a longer time, be prepared to accept that mamas might drop out as the study goes on. Generally, you will get more commitments to a shorter time frame. Reading several chapters a week might sound daunting to some mamas, but the good news is the chapters are short and easy reads.

   Encourage your members to dig in for the short term so they can experience the benefits in the long term!

   As for the duration of each meeting, this is entirely up to you, but anything longer than an hour per week might be a hindrance to some moms.

READ THE BOOK FIRST

Though reading first isn't mandatory to lead the group, you will feel more prepared if you read the book prior to starting the study. This will make it easier for you to facilitate group discussions and answer questions from your fellow mamas. If you're stepping up to lead this group, chances are you've already read the book. Fist bump, mama!

BE TRANSPARENT

If you have read the book, you know that I'm not shy about sharing my own frustrations and foibles as a mama. I get regular emails from readers who were encouraged by what I share, but the material will really start to sink in if mamas are willing to discuss with the group their own personal trials and triumphs. This might require you to take the lead to help create a space where mamas feel comfortable to share. The more your group is transparent about their journeys as mamas, the more you will get out of your study time. One point to consider here is confidentiality. Establishing an up-front rule that whatever is shared in the group stays only in the group will encourage more open discussions. It also helps the group stay accountable to one another and avoid the temptation of gossiping.

PRAY, PRAY, PRAY

Though this suggestion might seem obvious, it bears mentioning. Pray over your group. Pray to start and end each meeting. Leave time for prayer requests. Remember that one of the main points of the book is to apply biblical wisdom to raising our children. This can't be done without prayer...and lots of it. Ask God to reveal what He wants you to learn each week and how you can pray for others in the group.

In taking up CHRIST'S mantle of humility and gentleness, we lay down the right to cling to our overwhelm and the desire to have our struggles affirmed by our peers.

Notes

More Biblical Wisdom
for Mamas Like You

See how God can use the everyday trials of child raising to radically transform how you view hardship and grow you to become more like Jesus.

Humbly and gracefully rise to the high calling of motherhood without settling for mediocrity or losing your mind in the process.

ABOUT ABBIE

Abbie Halberstadt is a happy wife and mama of ten children, including two sets of identical twins. She's also a homeschool educator, fitness instructor, business owner, speaker, and writer. Through her blog and social media posts, she encourages women to dig deep to meet the challenges of everyday life. She, her husband, Shaun, and their children live in the Piney Woods of East Texas.

MIsForMama.net